To order additional copies of this contact us:
Margaret Sowemimo
P.O. Box 800
Powder Springs, GA 30127
678-949-8883 or

www.chosenremnant.org
Email: chosenremnant@gmail.com

Amazon.com

Printed in the USA
ISBN: 978-0-9752974-2-1

Other Books by the Author

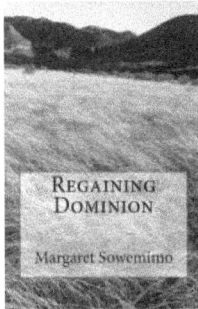

TABLE OF CONTENTS

ACKNOWLEDGEMENTS

To the persecuted Churches all over the world, I honor you. You are making Jesus known every day, and you stand for truth at the expense of your lives.

To the members of the Body of Christ all over the world, who also have chosen to remain steadfast and not compromise just so the church can grow, I honor you for your faithfulness.

My Jesus, I acknowledge your Lordship over my life and over Your Body. We know, no matter how challenging things may get, if we allow the Holy Spirit to lead your Church, the gates of hell cannot prevail against us as your Body.

To my Heavenly Father, thank you for sending Jesus.

To my family and friends, thank you for your financial support, prayer, and words of encouragement.

THE HEADLESS CHURCH

Preface

This book is about the vision the Lord showed me while I was in my prayer time and how the members of His Body are doing their own thing.

This book is not intended to condemn but to set you free to walk in the fullness of what God intends for your life. Whether you are a leader or a lay man, the book is for you. If you can discover where you are and realign to fit His purpose, the book will have done its job. It is about our aligning ourselves to the perfect will of God for our lives.

When I use the word Church, I am not referring to the building, but rather to you as a member of the Body of Christ. Without you in the building, it is just another building. We sometimes forget it is only a building, and we spend a lot of time and finances beautifying the physical building instead of the spiritual building, which we are!

⁹ For we are God's fellow workers; you are God's field, you are God's building.

1 Corinthians 3:9

The heart of God is to see the Church of Jesus Christ take her rightful place in the earth. We are Christ's ambassadors, and ambassadors represent their Nation or Kingdom well.

When Christ came, the Jews expected Him to take ruler-ship from the Romans through violence, but He shocked them when He made them understand that His Kingdom is not of their world. His ruler-ship transcends the present world.

We carry more authority than some of us realize. We are called to set the standard for the world, but, for the most part, today the world sets the standard for the Church. Becoming a seeker-friendly environment does not mean we water down the word of God, thereby lowering God's standard.

We are not capable of changing any man; it is only the Spirit of God that can convict a man. Your position is to preach the truth, leave Him to bring the conviction. You may sow the seed; someone else waters, but only God can give the increase.

We have less of the demonstration of the Spirit because we sometimes use any means possible to bring the people in. Some of our worship no longer focuses on Jesus.

The Holy Spirit is the only one that can bring conviction to a soul.

[8] And when He has come, He will convict the world of sin, and of righteousness, and of judgment: [9] of sin, because they do not believe in Me; [10] of righteousness, because I go to My Father and you see Me no more; [11] of judgment, because the ruler of this world is judged. [12] "I still have many things to say to you, but you cannot bear them now. [13] However, when He, the Spirit of truth, has come, He will guide you into all truth; for He will not speak on His own authority, but whatever He hears He will speak; and He will tell you things to come. [14] He will glorify Me, for He will take of what is Mine and declare it to you. [15] All things that the Father has are Mine. Therefore I said that He will take of Mine and declare it to you.

John 16:8-15

The persecuted churches have no fancy place to meet, but souls are won daily to the Kingdom. People are putting their lives on the line for the gospel daily. Their focus is on glorifying God and the Spirit of God backs them up with signs and wonders following.

"44 No one can come to Me unless the Father who sent Me draws him . . ."

John 6:44

Outside of the conviction of the Holy Spirit and God's kindness no one can change. Therefore we ought to stop trying to help God by devising gimmicks designed to bring people into the church. Our part is to preach the genuine gospel and let the Holy Spirit do His part.

If we, through our own craftiness, bring people into the Kingdom, they may be half-baked Christians. If what attracted them is no longer there, they will leave. However, if there is a true conversion through the power of the Holy Spirit, they will abide in Christ.

Peter on the day of Pentecost pointed the people to Jesus. He made them realize that all they had witnessed was because of Jesus. He preached a simple message, and three thousand people came to the Lord. The word of man cannot save, but the words inspired by the Holy Spirit will save and deliver.

Chapter 1

The Vision

During my prayer time, the Lord showed me a vision that disturbed me. I saw many headless people walking towards me. I staggered back because it looked so real. It seemed like they were going to walk right into me.

I asked the Lord what the vision meant. He said, "These people are part of My Church; they are going around headless because I am not the one leading them." He made me understand that the same way I moved away is the way the world pulls back from His church because we are doing what seems good in our sight.

When the Lord talks about the headless church, He is not talking about the building but the people found inside the building, the body of believers who worship in the building. There may be many denominations but as we all believe atonement is in the blood of Jesus and He is the Lord. You are part of His Body with Him being the HEAD. In the Old Testament, the Lord dwelt in the temple made by man, but in the New Testament God dwells in the heart of His people.

⁹ For we are God's fellow workers; you are God's field, you are God's building.
1 Corinthians 3:9

We cannot live solely on what He did in the past. We must be part of what He is doing now. Some of us stay comfortable in what used to work. No wonder we are not seeing God's moving in our midst as we should.

You cannot just copy what others did that worked for them, because that may not work for you. You have to be sure of the vision the Lord has given you–even though you can learn from what others have done. You have to align what you learn with what God has called you to do.

The children of Israel were told not to take more than the manna needed for each day. We cannot survive solely on what He did yesterday. We must press into Him for His Word for today. God knows what tomorrow will hold, so He is in the best position to direct us. God wants to be involved with our daily affairs.

The Prophetic Church will receive a word from the Lord and carry it out, but the Religious Church will stay stuck in what used to work. It is familiar territory, and, since it worked in the past, it is okay. The children of Israel carried around the snake pole that was used as a symbol for them to look upon when they were bitten by serpents because they had murmured against the Lord. Many had died from the venom. They carried it around for hundreds of years even though God was finished with the pole.

We cannot put new wine into an old wine skin. God does not want us to copy what another Church is doing; He wants us to follow His purpose for each Church.

If he wanted us all to be alike, He would have made us all the same. Each Church has a mandate from Him. He wants to lead the way. We cannot build for Him; He wants to initiate the building because He is the Master Builder.

Some want to live without restraint, claiming they are under grace. Christ paid the price, but grace is not a license for us to continue to live in sin. If we choose to live in sin, we move from under His covering (Headship). If I claim to be a new creation, but I still continue to live the way I used to, it means old things have not passed away. I cannot feel comfortable living the way I used to. It should be the same for you: You no longer should enjoy the life of sin. Otherwise, what sets you and me apart from the unsaved? Paul said it well in Romans 6

1 "What shall we say then? Shall we continue in sin that grace may abound? 2 Certainly not! How shall we who died to sin live any longer in it?"

Romans 6:1-2

For the power of God to flow, the unclean will have to go. There can be no power when we live contrary to His word. Holiness unto the Lord is still in the Bible, and it applies to the Church of Jesus Christ even though we are under grace.

The Church is quickly losing her influence because we are more concerned with looking right in society than looking right in the sight of God. We dress nice, we preach well, we entertain well, but people go home still bearing the issues they came with.

We attend many seminars on church growth and different aspects of ministry, but few seminars on coming to spend three days in the presence of God where we seek His face and pray for the salvation of souls and for the power of the spirit to bring conviction to the people in our city and environment.

Where is the power of God today? This question is on the lips of many people. We are to go back to the old landmark to be able to see the result we want to see. I am guilty of leaving God out sometimes, as you probably do, too. There are certain things we feel we are capable of doing, and they seem like the right thing to do because Church A did it and it worked for them. God may have given that to Church A based on their mandate.

Moses was instructed by God to hit the rock to get water for the children of Israel. He obeyed God by hitting the rock but the next time around, he was told to speak to the rock—but he hit the rock again. Even though God honored Himself by bringing water out of the rock, it cost Moses his chance of entering the Promised Land.

The Lord is serious about obedience. You must NEVER take God for granted if you want to succeed in ministry. As an individual or as a ministry, taking God for

granted will lead us into religion instead of
revelation.

*⁷ Then the Lord spoke to Moses,
saying, ⁸ "Take the rod; you and your
brother Aaron gather the congregation
together. Speak to the rock before their eyes,
and it will yield its water; thus you shall
bring water for them out of the rock, and
give drink to the congregation and their
animals." ⁹ So Moses took the rod from
before the Lord as He commanded him.
¹⁰ And Moses and Aaron gathered the
assembly together before the rock; and he
said to them, "Hear now, you rebels! Must
we bring water for you out of this
rock?" ¹¹ Then Moses lifted his hand and
struck the rock twice with his rod; and water
came out abundantly, and the congregation
and their animals drank. ¹² Then
the Lord spoke to Moses and Aaron,
"Because you did not believe Me, to hallow
Me in the eyes of the children of Israel,
therefore you shall not bring this assembly
into the land which I have given them."
¹³ This was the water of Meribah, because
the children of Israel contended with
the Lord, and He was hallowed among them.*

Numbers 20:7-13

The rock, we were told by Paul in 1 Corinthians 10:4, was Christ. Jesus was to be smitten once for our iniquity, but striking the rock a second time meant He was being smitten twice.

Moses, in verse 10 of the scripture, voiced his frustration with the people by calling them rebels. He even went on to say, "Must we bring water for you from out of the rock?" Moses had no ability to bring water out of the rock, but, at this point in time, he placed himself and Aaron in the position of those who would provide the water.

The Lord promised He would build His church, and the gates of hell will not prevail against the church. We can then say, if we build the church for God, the gates of hell may prevail against the church.

Some churches dim the light to create a less threatening environment for the unbeliever. When you go into the physician's office for examination, they do not dim the light or take away things that would allow you to know what they stand for. The TV in the waiting room has health related shows, and they admonish you not to change the channel. This has not stopped you from going there for your checkups. Why then do we have to change who we are because we want the unbeliever to be comfortable?

The Church must not water down or sugar coat the gospel message just because you want the unbeliever to be comfortable. The word of God discerns the thought and intent of the heart. If you just preach what God gives you to preach, the Spirit of God will convict those who need to be convicted and encourage those who need to be encouraged. The word of God is powerful enough to do that.

I believe anyone who comes to the church of his own volition is looking for something that could not be found in the world. Let us look at two churches: One has 200 members with 180 people born again, compared to a church with 3000 and 600 people born again. Although it looks like the church with 600 have more people, percentage-wise only 20% of the people are believers, while the one with the 200 has 90% believers.

We are in crucial times, and only a church that is led by the Spirit of God will survive the times we are in.

We cannot move into what God wants us to do if we do not move away from what we want to do. A fleshly-led church cannot be Spirit-led at the same time. The Holy Spirit is not going to share His position with anyone else. Flesh cannot glory in the sight of the Lord.

The Spirit led church will not be preoccupied with many activities that satisfy the flesh and not the spirit.

There is nothing wrong in a congregation engaging in activities that enable them to build relationships in the congregation. But when the motive is to use all things possible to get the people to come to church in order to have a large congregation, it breaks the Lord's heart, because you are taking over His role as the Master Builder. It means you cannot trust Him to fulfill His promise of building His Church.

Some people attend every conference in town but have no personal devotional time with the Lord.

This type of person falls prey to the deception of the enemy. They run off with everything they are told without lining things up with scripture. You will remain Headless unless you retrace your path and spend some time in His presence ALONE.

Some of these things we do because we do not want to pay the price for intimacy with the Lord. They hope they can become more anointed by attending conferences and getting hands laid on them.

The Power of God is not a magic wand that can be waved and boom, you have it. There is a price to pay. Some of the people you try to go to paid a price to be where they are in God. It is total surrender in which you must acknowledge His Lordship over your life.

Jesus, the Son of God; took time out to commune with the Father. Before His earthly ministry began, He went apart for forty days to seek the face of the Father in preparation. Why then do we think we do not need to pay any price spiritually to see the manifestation of His power? Some just take the revelation God gave others and run with it.

Unless we as the church of Jesus Christ change, the world cannot change, no one will see our light. As the light, we should brighten up our environment, but if I am still in the dark myself, how can people see me and glorify God? I want to take my orders from Him. The more we try to follow Him,

the clearer His voice becomes and the more
we see the Bible as our ultimate guide.

Chapter 2

The Naaman-Mindset Church:

Pride

They have an air of superiority about them.

Naaman was a man of prestige who led the Syrian army, but he was a leper. During one of their raids, they captured a young girl from Israel. She told Naaman's wife about Elisha, the prophet in Israel, whom God could use to cure him of the leprosy. Naaman was told, and he went with a letter from his own king to the king of Israel.

[6] *"Then he brought the letter to the king of Israel, which said, Now be advised, when this letter comes to you, that I have sent Naaman my servant to you, that you may heal him of his leprosy.* [7] *And it happened, when the king of Israel read the letter, that he tore his clothes and said, "Am I God, to kill and make alive, that this man sends a man to me to heal him of his leprosy?*

*Therefore please consider, and see how he
seeks a quarrel with me." ⁸ So it was, when
Elisha the man of God heard that the king of
Israel had torn his clothes that he sent to the
king saying, "Why have you torn your
clothes? Please let him come to me, and he
shall know that there is a prophet in Israel."*

2 Kings 5:6-8

The king of Syria thought he could just send
a letter to demand a cure for Naaman. The
king of Israel was concerned because he
knew he did not have the ability to cure
Naaman. Elisha sent for Naaman.

Naaman came to meet the prophet but was
not pleased that Elisha did not come out to
meet him, the head of the Syrian army.
Second, Elisha sent his messenger to him
with instruction for him to wash in the
Jordan River.

This instruction seemed too simple—and
was humiliating, too. Naaman felt he could
have gone back to his country to dip in the
Abanah and the Pharpar, rivers of
Damascus. But, of course, if he had done
that, he would have remained a leper.

Naaman had money, wealth, and position but that did not change the fact that he was a leper. If Naaman were just an ordinary person, he may have been kept outside of normal society.

The Church of Laodicea in the book of Revelation saw themselves as rich and felt they needed nothing, but Jesus saw them as wretched and in need. If he had not sent a message to the church, they would not have seen the need for change.

14 "And to the angel of the church of the Laodiceans write, ' These things says the Amen, the Faithful and True Witness, the Beginning of the creation of God: 15 "I know your works, that you are neither cold nor hot. I could wish you were cold or hot. 16 So then, because you are lukewarm, and neither cold nor hot, I will vomit you out of My mouth. 17 Because you say, 'I am rich, have become wealthy, and have need of nothing'—and do not know that you are wretched, miserable, poor, blind, and naked— 18 I counsel you to buy from Me gold refined in the fire, that you may be rich; and white garments, that you may be clothed, that the shame of your nakedness may not be revealed; and anoint your eyes with eye salve, that you may see. [19] As many as I love, I rebuke and chasten. Therefore be zealous and repent."

Revelation 3:14-19

If Naaman had not met the young girl they took from Israel, he would have remained a rich leper. Some of the members of the Body of Christ have structure without the power. Everything flows well in the service. Things are done the same way from week to week; people come and go back the way they came. The building is wonderful; the whole service is wonderful; but no place was actually allowing the Spirit of God to move. God may want to start when we are finishing, but, because of our insensitivity, we may miss His plan for the day.

Naaman had his own idea of how the healing should take place. We feel like that too sometimes; we feel we know how God will be moving and we try to help Him out.

With the encouragement from Naaman's maid, Naaman went to the Jordan river and dipped in it until he was fully cleansed. He then professed there is no other God but the God of Israel. Our number one priority as a member of His Body is to make Him known. What Elisha did for Naaman did not draw attention to Elisha but to God. Today there may have been a press conference to interview Elisha or a movie in His name. There is nothing wrong with being appreciated for what God is doing in our lives as long as we point others back to Jesus.

The Jordan River is not what cured Naaman. I am sure many people had dipped in the Jordan in the past but were never healed. It was Naaman's obedience to the word of the Lord that cleansed him of the leprosy.

10 And Elisha sent a messenger to him, saying, "Go and wash in the Jordan seven times, and your flesh shall be restored to you, and you shall be clean." 11 But Naaman became furious, and went away and said, "Indeed, I said to myself, 'He will surely come out to me, and stand and call on the name of the Lord his God, and wave his hand over the place, and heal the leprosy.' 12 Are not the Abanah and the Pharpar, the rivers of Damascus, better than all the waters of Israel? Could I not wash in them and be clean?" So he turned and went away in a rage. 13 And his servants came near and spoke to him, and said, "My father, if the prophet had told you to do something great, would you not have done it? How much more then, when he says to you, 'Wash, and be clean'?" ¹⁴ So he went down and dipped seven times in the Jordan, according to the saying of the man of God; and his flesh was restored like the flesh of a little child, and he was clean.¹⁵ And he returned to the man of God, he and all his aides, and came and stood before him; and he said, "Indeed, now I know that there is no God in all the earth, except in Israel; now therefore, please take a gift from your servant."

2 Kings 5:.10-15

A word from the Lord brought about a permanent change for the better in Naaman's life. For us today a word from the Lord, carried out in obedience, will get the church further than what any seminar or activity would do.

The Naaman-type Church today is very proud of their achievements; they have money and big buildings. They do not see the need to consult with God on issues anymore: If it looks good, it is fine to do it, because it will bring in more people.

The complaint of Naaman did not get Elisha to come out and meet him. Naaman was looking for something that the God of Elisha can give. He had to follow the instruction or go back the way he came. The church cannot compromise. I said earlier, someone who comes to the church in the way Naaman went to Elisha is looking for something. Compromise is not going to give it to them. If we follow the Lord's instruction, we will get the God result.

Our boast should not be in our accomplishment but in the relationship we have with the Lord. We should be more interested in what God can accomplish in the lives of His people than just filling the building. The King of Israel became perplexed when he saw the letter. He knew he was not equipped for that, but thank God for the Prophet Elisha whom God used.

Ultimately we want them to be able to say after God touches them that there is no God like our God. This can only happen if we let Him lead

Chapter 3

Fellowship with God:
Seek Him!

God wanted fellowship, so He created man. Man stepped outside of God's protection by disobeying God's instruction not to eat from the Tree of Knowledge of Good and Evil. Eating of the Tree meant man will know good from evil but will not be able to help himself.

The Church is coming to the age in which knowledge is increasing but the knowledge is not helping the spirit man. We are enlightening the mind, while the spirit man is starving.

Someone asked me a while ago if I had heard of 60/40 sharing, and I had no clue. It was then explained to me thus: A pastor brings in a guest speaker and they both agree that at the end of the message, he will cajole the people to sow a seed, which they both will share at the end of the ministration. The visiting minister will take 60% while the home pastor takes 40%. I was shocked to hear this. Where is the fear of God?

It is also sad to hear what the Prophetic Ministry has become in some quarters. It is now a tool to manipulate God's people in some places. People are interested in hearing something from the heart of God that will encourage or set them free.

Some "Prophets" now send people beforehand to gather information about people in the congregation they are about to visit. They come in to the meeting calling out car number, street number, and different things. Some people are taken in by this, ignorant of the fact that it was prearranged. This happened to the friend of the pastor of one of the churches where I ministered.

Some consult with the occultist for power because they want to move in the prophetic.

Some years ago a sister at the church I attended at the time stopped me to tell me she had something she wanted to discuss with me. I told her to call me at home. She called and what came out of her mouth was "I want power." I did not understand what that had to do with me. I told her, "So what has that got to do with me?" She said she wanted God to use her like He was using me. I was confused because I believed she was matured enough to know every perfect gift is given by God through the Holy Spirit.

I told her I did not have the ability to do that. I encouraged her to cultivate her relationship with the Lord, because what she wants is attainable if she spends time with God. She wanted to be able to flow in the prophetic but was not willing to pay the price. The gifts are a by-product of loving God, the giver of the gifts.

I must say there are some prophets that are genuine and do move in strong revelation, words of wisdom, and knowledge. These are the prophets who seek the face of God. God sees them, and He will reward them for their purity.

The dear sister wanted to move in the gift but was not willing to give the time required seeking the face of God, who is the giver of the gift.

People who go the diabolical way will not be held guiltless before God. We have to be careful what we take in and where we go.

This is why it is important to spend time with God. Have an intimate relationship. The Lord wants to tell you His plan for your life before He tells someone else.

Some members of the Body of Christ are running from one seminar to another, seeking how to become the best person they can be. They are busy running around to learn how to become rich. It is God who gives us the power to make wealth. My question to you is this: How much time do you spend seeking God and winning souls?

30 Now if God so clothes the grass of the field, which today is, and tomorrow is thrown into the oven, will He not much more clothe you, O you of little faith? 31 "Therefore do not worry, saying, 'What shall we eat?' or 'What shall we drink?' or 'What shall we wear?' 32 For after all these things the Gentiles seek. For your heavenly Father knows that you need all these things. 33 But seek first the kingdom of God and His righteousness, and all these things shall be added to you.

Matthew 6:30-33

Do not get me wrong, I know we need the money, but it is not supposed to be our all-consuming passion. It may be challenging at first, but, as you give more time to Kingdom work, rest assured that God will eventually reward you. God is not going to let you lack when you focus on doing His work first.

24 "No one can serve two masters; for either he will hate the one and love the other, or else he will be loyal to the one and despise the other. You cannot serve God and mammon.

Matthew 6:24

We are busy laying up treasure for ourselves here on earth, forgetting what the scripture says in Matthew 6:19-21. We should not lay up treasures for ourselves here. Anything could happen, and it would be gone in a minute. If God should ask you today to give up all that you have and you cannot do that, those things have taken His place.

19 "Do not lay up for yourselves treasures on earth, where moth and rust destroy and where thieves break in and steal, 20 but lay up for yourselves treasures in heaven, where neither moth nor rust destroys and where thieves do not break in and steal. 21 For where your treasure is, there your heart will be also. **Matthew 6:19-21**

I had a discussion with a prominent man of God in which he shared with me how he thought he could give up anything for God. He said now the Lord has really blessed him and settled him. The Lord one day asked him how he would feel if He chose to uproot him and take him to another country.

He said he told the Lord not to do that. He immediately thought of what it would be like starting again. He said he could not believe he would react that way. I have been there myself and saw how easy it is to say, but doing is another thing.

God asked Solomon to name one thing he would like. Solomon asked for wisdom to rule God's people, and, because he asked for wisdom, God also gave Solomon great wealth.

[7] In that night God appeared to Solomon, and said to him, "Ask what I shall give you." [8] And Solomon said to God, "You have shown great and steadfast love to David my father, and have made me king in his place. [9] O LORD God, let your word to David my father be now fulfilled, for you have made me king over a people as numerous as the dust of the earth. [10] Give me now wisdom and knowledge to go out and come in before

this people, for who can govern this people of yours, which is so great?" [11] God answered Solomon, "Because this was in your heart, and you have not asked possessions, wealth, honor, or the life of those who hate you, and have not even asked long life, but have asked wisdom and knowledge for yourself that you may govern my people over whom I have made you king, [12] wisdom and knowledge are granted to you. I will also give you riches, possessions, and honor, such as none of the kings had who were before you, and none after you shall have the like."

1 Chronicles 1:7-12

God blessed Solomon with things he did not ask for because he focused on what was important to God. Being King over Israel was not going to be easy without the wisdom of God. Solomon knew He could not lead without God being the leader.

This reminds me of Moses in Exodus 33:15-16, where Moses said that if God's presence were not going to go with them, they were not to be brought into the Land. Moses knew that without the presence of God they could not attain the inheritance. The Church cannot survive for long without His presence. It is in Him we live and move and have our being.

God gave Solomon some instructions on what not to do. He was not to marry foreign women or import horses from Egypt. Solomon did these things, and it cost him the loss of ten of the twelve tribes of Israel.

We should learn from this, too. We are to obey His instruction to seek His Kingdom first. Some prophets are more interested in the people coming to them for a word instead of teaching the people how to hear and commune with God for themselves.

The pastor is not willing to release the people to go and do the will of God. Some pastors have become kings instead of fathers. True fathers want their children to do better than they have done. True pastors are willing to release the sheep that is ready to go and fulfill the plan of God with a father's blessing, as well as support them in any way they can.

We also have the sheep that feels he knows more than the shepherd that is over them and is ready to release himself to go ahead and start a ministry even though he is not ready. But, because the sheep is gifted, he feels he can make it work. If God has not released you to go but you go anyway, you may abort His vision for you. You become headless because you have now run ahead of Him.

If God has released you to go and you face challenges, it does not mean God is not in it, it just means you are on the right track—but facing enemy opposition. The vision will eventually unfold. Stay encouraged. Do not give up.

Since we started Harvestland International Christian Center, per the Lord's instruction, it has been one opposition after another. But we see these difficulties as a sign that we are going in the right direction. We are not running to the safety of anyone, but into the arms of the Lord where we find true safety.

We have to move away from the Naaman mentality that we have our own idea of how to run things. What will help you is to spend time in God's presence and with people that are passionate about the things of God. You can hear His heart and get your instruction from Him. If Naaman had stuck with this mindset, he would not have gained his deliverance.

Chapter 4

The Lame Man at
Gate Beautiful

Peter and John were at the gate Beautiful. They saw the lame man at his usual post (Acts 3). He was probably wondering how many people would give him alms for the day. Would he get more than what he got yesterday? It undoubtedly never crossed his mind that he would receive a miracle..

He had settled into life the way it was, collecting alms for a living. He settled for man determining his own destiny.

Peter and John told him to look at them, which would have been different for him. People just dropped things in the plate. What could be making this one different, why does he need to look at them?

The church today should be able to tell the world, "Look at us. We have what you need for redemption. We are the answer to what they are seeking. The silver and the gold that men are running after cannot satisfy." Getting the alms was not satisfying. Walking is! We cannot remain spiritually lame; we have to rise up and walk. You cannot continue to depend on someone else to take care of your spiritual need. You have to allow the Holy Spirit to free you to experience a more fulfilling life.

Some of our buildings are like the gate Beautiful, with a lame spiritual atmosphere. The activities are so structured that there is no room for the Holy Spirit to move. If we allow The Spirit to move, it will throw off the schedule. We have to get in and out to make room for the next service because people do not want to stay too long.

When God is moving, it is usually as if time stands still, because no one wants to leave. The people are so refreshed in His presence that they just want to stay there. But that will not be possible because room must be made for the next service. I pray God will sometimes just disrupt our agenda.

I can think of an instance when we were in worship, and the presence of God was so strong that I perceived in my spirit that worship was all God wanted from us for that day. I slipped a note to my pastor to let us continue with the worship if he felt led. He was so happy for the confirmation. He said he felt the same way but was concerned the people might not like the idea of just worship and no sermon for the day. He went with the worship, and, needless to say, we all left the service refreshed and fulfilled.

My husband and I both pastor a church now. There are days we come into a service and the Lord changes the order of service. We have learned to flow as He leads.

We have to be careful that the church does not become lame. The lame man received alms every week. He stayed at the gate with his plate reaching out as people walked into the temple. For him, begging had become his lifestyle, and he was okay doing it since there was no other way out.

It is time for the Church of Jesus Christ to arise from her slumber so that we can enjoy the abundant life He purchased for us with His blood. Become the conduit through which the world will experience the signs and the wonders that come with the presence of the Lord.

Peter and John told the lame man that they had no money to give him. Can you imagine what must have gone through the lame man's mind when they said that, before hearing the rest of the sentence?

They commanded him to rise in the name of Jesus Christ of Nazareth. They carried the anointing which silver and gold cannot purchase. He had been doing the same thing over and over, but, for the first time in His life, he received something greater than money—a permanent solution to His problem.

That is different! They had something to give that money could not buy. He rose, probably forgetting his alms plate as he leapt up praising God. There is more to what God can do in your life and in my life.

The place was called "Beautiful." The word means a place that has the ability to give great pleasure, a delightful place. However, for this lame man, all the pleasure he derived was collecting alms, and he had settled for that. On this fateful day, he experienced Beautiful for the first time in his life.

The gate really lived up to its name for the first time ever in this lame man's life. When you have a genuine encounter with God's presence, you cannot remain the same. Moses came from the mountain and no one could look at his face because it radiated the glory of God.

One of the experiences I have had with the Lord was feeling His heartbeat. I felt His heart connected to mine, and I saw the perishing souls, millions, before my eyes. I felt the compassion God has for His creation.

The experience left me crying for days. I could not relay the experience without wanting to cry.

Peter took the lame man by the right hand and lifted him up. Peter professed that it was in the name of Jesus of Nazareth that the man would walk. He followed by raising the man by the right hand because he knew the miracle would take place. Some of us are in places where we are satisfied when The Lord desires to thrust you into greater things. He is ready to do much more with your life. He wants people to see His glory. The place the man stayed was a prominent place and people had gotten used to seeing him there. God knew what would happen that day. Attention would be drawn to Jesus after the miracle. Many had seen the lame man and knew him well.

The man did not go and meet them in a building; they saw him at the gate and ministered to him. Whether we are in the building or outside the building, as the church we carry His presence. Therefore, we should cause a change wherever we go.

We are not seeing much of the manifestation of His power in the lives of His people again because some are building the kingdom of man instead of the Kingdom of God.

If you see a Church that is totally submitted to the Lordship of Jesus Christ, even though they may be few, His manifest presence will always be there. You will leave the meeting refreshed while still reflecting on the service even after you get home.

I do not know about you, but I would rather be with a small group that is experiencing the presence of God than a mega group with nothing happening. If it is found among a mega group, praise God. We must not just play church; we must encounter Him in our services.

At the command of Peter and John, the lame man stood and entered the temple with them—walking, leaping, and praising God. The people saw him walking and praising God.

They carried the anointing, knew their authority, gave the word of command, and followed it up with action. There was no fanfare; the focus was on Jesus as the healer.

Then they knew that it was he who sat begging alms at the Beautiful Gate of the temple; and they were filled with wonder and amazement at what had happened to him. **(Acts 3:8-10 NKJV)**

The story does not stop there, because many more in different places would hear about what happened to him and the man himself would spread the news.

God does not build the church by our agenda and what we can do. How many seminars did Peter and John attend on church growth? None. They spent time with the Master Builder. It was out of that relationship that the church grew.

I believe God has assigned people to certain churches based upon their need, but if we continue to use gimmicks to bring them in, we end up attracting the wrong types of people

The gold and the silver are not what will do it. The man was sustained by gold and silver that he received at the Beautiful Gate, but it could not help to make him whole. He needed the touch from the Master.

The church of Jesus Christ was not redeemed by gold or silver but by His precious blood. It is in the blood that we find redemption. By the stripes that He took we received healing and wholeness. Unless you walk in that which He has ordained you for, you cannot be whole.

It is when we let Him build His church that we will see the fullness of the harvest. Though the man was at the Beautiful Gate, he was still lame.

When we let the Master Builder do the construction, it will be perfectly done. It is not going to look like anything we can do. Peter and John were ordinary men used in an extraordinary way. They carried something that most people who came daily did not have; otherwise, they would not have been able to help the man.

The Church of Jesus just needs to follow the command of the Master. If the Church does not spend time seeking Him and developing real intimacy, we will not see the manifestation of His glory.

It is easier to move around from one seminar to another seminar learning about Church growth because you have the steps to follow. What is the essence of growth if the power of God is not present? People need to grow more in love with Jesus. That should be the main focus. It is out of the flow of that relationship that things happen. Allow God to be God in your life and ministry, and He will do great things.

When He touches a life in a miraculous way, the news will spread abroad. Many will come because of the testimony.

I am not against going to seminars, but if that is what you are placing your trust, in order to grow your church, you may grow numerically but not as spiritually sound. If you leave it to the Lord to build His church, there will be real people filling your church and seeking a real God.

Follow the churches where Christ is the center and you find people waiting outside the door to get in, because the people know God will do something to touch them. They may not know how, but the assurance is there that He will touch them.

I read about a woman of God whose meetings started at 9 a.m., but people were already at the door by 5 a.m. waiting for the door to open. This is what happens when we focus on Jesus.

The disciples were first called Christians in Antioch because they acted like Jesus. They did miracles as He did.

Sinners are not supposed to interact with His church and leave the way they came. A church stopped the yearly memorization of the Bible because they did not want the unbeliever to be intimidated. Who says a verse in the passage to be memorized is not what will minister to the person? We are not to lower our standards for the world.

The church is not a place for the unbeliever to be comfortable; it is a place to bring conviction. A sinner who walks into a church is looking for something. The person knows what church is about. It means he/she is yearning for something. The word of the Lord is what discerns the thought and the intent of the heart. It is where a sinner can find hope and deliverance.

At the garden Jesus asked the Father to take the cup of His suffering away if it were possible; "Nevertheless, not my will but your will be done." The church of Jesus is not about our will, but about His will being done. He said, "I only do and speak the things that my Father tells me."

How many of us as His church can say today, "I only do what the Father tells me"? How many pastors can truly say, "The things I do in the church are based on what He tells me"?

I have no issue with learning and acquiring knowledge, but that must not take precedence over the voice of God.

The Church can only become a place without spot or wrinkle if we allow Christ as the Head to lead His church.

27That He might present her to Himself a glorious church, not having spot or wrinkle or any such thing, but that she should be holy and without blemish.

Ephesians 5:27

If Christ is the Head of His Church, the Spirit of Christ will be the one directing the affairs of the Church. The scripture says "as many as are led by the Spirit of God are the sons of God." It means if we are not allowing the Spirit of God to lead, we cannot claim to be the sons of God. Ouch, that hurts, but we cannot serve two masters; we will love one and hate the other.

The lady who followed Paul spoke with accuracy, "These are the servants of the Most High that have come to show us the way of salvation." A church that is not discerning, if that had happened today, would have put a signpost out and have a commercial on TV; with her testifying, the spirit behind the message would have been missed.

No wonder Jesus said some will come and say, "I prophesied in your name. I did miracles in your name," and He would say to them, "Depart from me you that work iniquity."

How can we do things in His name and still be rejected by Him? It will be because it was all done for the wrong motive.

A Church can do great and mighty things in His name but if He did not call her to that, it will be wasted time and the works will burn at the time of receiving rewards.

The Lord told me during my prayer time one day that "If I send you to reach a hundred and you go after the thousand, you would have done a good thing—but not the God thing." This means that this work will burn in the fire and there will be no reward. It is possible that the small crowd in which a person is being sent is where the next world evangelist is.

Ministers are seeking help from powers of darkness because they want to grow the church. Because of the one miracle at the Gate Beautiful, five thousand people were added to the church through the message Peter gave after the miracle (Acts 4:4).

Peter used the miracle of the lame man as an in-road to preach the gospel. If we focus on loving Him and reaching the lost, He will give us what we need to function as His Church.

Some of us as His church need to repent, because we are busy doing this and that to bring in money. I understand the Church needs the finances to be able to make the ministry function; but who says He has not made provision for what He has asked you to do? When Jesus needed to pay taxes, He sent Peter to catch the first fish and in its mouth he found the money needed.

George Mueller was an evangelist who ran his orphanage on faith. This excerpt was taken from Christianity.com:

"The children are dressed and ready for school. But there is no food for them to eat," the housemother of the orphanage informed George Mueller. George asked her to take the 300 children into the dining room and have them sit at the tables.
He thanked God for the food and waited.
George knew God would provide food for the children as he always did. *Within minutes, a baker knocked on the door. "Mr. Mueller," he said, "last night I could not sleep. Somehow I knew that you would need bread this morning. I got up and baked three batches for you. I will bring it in."*

*Soon, there was another knock at the door.
It was the milkman. His cart had broken
down in front of the orphanage. The milk
would spoil by the time the wheel was fixed.
He asked George if he could use some free
milk. George smiled as the milkman brought
in ten large cans of milk. It was just enough
for the 300 thirsty children."*

This shows me that if we stay within the
boundaries of what He has called us to do,
we will not lack. It may not come right
away, but be rest assured He will be on time.

Let me share this testimony to encourage
you. We just started the church. A young
lady came with her son. We had juice and
peanuts but knew we could not give the
toddler peanuts. We gave him the drink
without a snack.

I purposed to get some snacks for children
for next Sunday. At least three people
suggested we buy Gold Fish crackers. We
usually go shopping for the things on Friday.

On Wednesday afternoon, the postman came
with a big box for us in the mail. We were
not expecting a package, but it was

addressed to us. We opened the package—
and what was inside was Gold Fish
crackers!

The person who sent it was a friend's
daughter who lives in Texas (we are in
Georgia). She said their company had a free
box they had no need for, and she felt it
might be useful for our children's ministry.

Wow is all we could say! She knew nothing
about what transpired on Sunday, but God
knew. He sent it on Wednesday, two days
before we were to go shopping for the
crackers. God is still The Provider. Let us
learn to trust Him instead of leaning on our
own understanding.

"Trust in the Lord with all your heart,
And lean not on your own understanding;
⁶ In all your ways acknowledge Him, And He
shall direct your paths.
                    Proverbs 3:5-6
The challenge comes when I become
presumptuous and start doing things He did
not call me to do.

George Mueller had no funds to provide the
meal for the children, but God met the need.
Imagine the cart of the milkman breaking
down in front of the orphanage. An angel

must have held on to the wheel of the cart (smile!)

Some ministers are on TV today when God may have wanted them to do something else. Media is good, and it is not a problem if we are actually called to the radio or the TV.

If the Lord asks you why you do what you do, what would your answer be? Would it be because others are doing it or because you believe He asked you to do it?

Regardless of how blessed the ministry is and whether funding is no issue, maybe instead of being on TV, He wants you to channel the money towards something else. But, you think, other ministries are on TV, so why not mine?

I am guilty of doing things or starting on something before seeking His face and sometimes I am able to stop in my tracks and seek His direction. But other times I have gone ahead and done something and I had to repent. He speaks to us in different ways.

Anything the flesh touches seems to live but will eventually die. Anything the Spirit touches may seem to die but it will live to bring forth much fruit.

We are to come into His presence with thanksgiving in our hearts, but instead the flesh wants to come before His presence with our agenda on our hearts.

I was at a service once and this prophet who used to walk with such purity as a young prophet came and ministered to the people. Towards the end he said, "There are people here who are to give a thousand," and, when they gave, he prophesied over them.

He then called for five hundred dollars. Those came, too, and he prophesied, but to a lesser degree.

He went down until he got to those that had fifty dollars. To these he gave a pat in the back saying, "God bless you."
The blessing of God is really what one needs to prosper but, in this situation, he said that because they did not have much to give, he did not have any prophetic word for them.

Something similar happened at another meeting I attended. The minister made a similar altar call, but, when he got to those who gave fifty dollars, he sang, "And now let the weak say I am strong; let the poor say I am rich because of what the Lord has done for us; give thanks."

The lady with the widow's mite, Jesus said, gave more than the others because she gave out of her need. These people also could have given all they had. When did we start giving prophetic word based on the size of a person's offering?

Leaders should avoid manipulating people into giving. God loves a cheerful giver, and you want people to give from the heart, not because they are coerced into giving.

Both the leader and the members of the congregation are all part of His Church, and everyone needs to grow in the art of hearing God for himself or herself. You have to check what you are hearing to make sure your spirit is at peace with it.

This testimony from a lady really blessed me. She said whenever she is dressing, she will ask the Lord if it is ok to wear what she was about to wear. One day, the Lord told her to wear a blue dress that she did not like and had not worn in a long time.

She knew it had to be the Lord because she would not have chosen that dress to wear. She wore the dress and, when she got to the place where she normally takes the bus, a lady walked up to her, narrated her situation and how the voice had told her she would see a lady in blue at the bus stop that would help her.

She was able to help the lady. What if she had disobeyed the voice that told her to wear blue? She would have missed the divine appointment that the Lord had for her. God is still speaking and leading His people by His Spirit.

I was to have dinner with a friend and she called to ask if her friend could come with her. I told her it was okay!

She asked if I could minster to the friend when l met with them. I promised to pray for the lady before we met so as to know the heart of God concerning her.

He gave me some words for her. I always make it a point to take a gift to someone l am meeting with for the first time, so I inquired of the Lord what to get her, and he laid a scarf on my heart. I asked for what color and I believe I heard baby blue.

While we were waiting for the food to be served, I noticed the place was very cold and she had on a short sleeve dress and was shivering. I usually give the gift when we are about to leave, but in this case I broke my protocol because l did not have an extra scarf. The lady's friend, too, had a scarf around her neck. I took out the scarf and gave it to this lady I was meeting to shield her from the cold.

She covered herself with it. She got up to show us the trimming at the end of her dress, it was baby blue. Anyone seeing her dress and the scarf would think she had bought the scarf for the dress.

This lady had been under such condemnation because of her past lifestyle that she just could not get past it. The Lord gave me **Romans 8:33** while I was praying for her.

33 Who shall bring a charge against God's elect? It is God who justifies.

I believed God had something to say to her through the scripture. While I was ministering to her, she began crying, not caring that she was at the restaurant. It was after the ministration that I found out about the guilt she still carried around.

She left knowing God had touched her. If I had not taken the time to seek the face of the Lord on her behalf, we would have had a good lunch, but she would have left the way she came.

Some may say "this is too much or spooky." It is not at all. You can be as intimate with God as you want. You can stay in the shallow end of the pool or dare to venture to the deep end knowing there is a life saver there. David asked God where to move to, and God told him Judah. David went on to ask where in Judah and God told him, "Hebron."

"It happened after this that David inquired of the Lord, saying, "Shall I go up to any of the cities of Judah?" And the Lord said to him, "Go up." David said, "Where shall I go up?" And He said, "To Hebron."

2 Samuel 2:1

He wants to be in command of His people. He loads us with benefits daily so we can be true blessing for the people He leads us to.

The church needs to awake from her slumber. It is when we let Him reign that the earth will be filled with the knowledge of His glory.

King Jehoshaphat was to go to war with Ahab; they called for the prophets, and all of them said it was okay to go.

Thank God King Jehoshaphat was discerning. He asked to see if there was another prophet they could inquire from. Ahab said, "Yes there is a prophet of God who never says anything good about me." Well, Micah came and said, if they went, Ahab would be killed. King Ahab did not believe him; he went—and he died during the war. **(1 Kings 22)**

Prophets of God, it is time to speak the heart of God and not what the people want to hear; we are the mouthpiece of God to His people. We speak what He wants us to speak, not speak what will tickle the ears of the people.

Speaking the truth may mean no honorarium. Speaking a lie as prophesy may bring in a big honorarium, but one would have walked in disobedience.

Every minister must not lose sight of God
being the rewarder of those who persistently
seek Him. He will use a man to bless you,
but you must allow Him to use the vessel He
has prepared instead of getting in His way
by trying to devise means to get people to
bless you.

He prepared the widow of Zarephath for
Elijah (1 King 17). He prepared the childless
Shunammite woman for Elisha (2 Kings 4).
He prepared the colt for Jesus. If the church
can have faith in the finished work of Christ,
we can become the Church He wants us to
be.

We release our natural ability to Him, so
that He can make it supernatural ability. It is
then we can do exploit. He wants the world
to see His supernatural ability working in us
and through us.

Peter was an unlearned fisherman, and so
were most of the others, but, when it came
to moving in power, he spoke with great
authority and boldness.

Chapter 5

The Davidic-Mindset Church:

Worshiper

David was a shepherd who, at a very young age, looked after his father's sheep. He was bold because he fought the lion and the bear when they attacked the sheep, and he killed them.

David was about his father's business without looking for recognition. He was diligent not because the father was watching him, but because David knew a true shepherd cares for the sheep.

God in heaven saw all that David did; He saw his boldness and dedication. He called him out of the field to shepherd His people.

11 And Samuel said to Jesse, "Are all the young men here?" Then he said, "There remains yet the youngest, and there he is, keeping the sheep." And Samuel said to Jesse, "Send and bring him. For we will not

sit down till he comes here." ¹² So he sent
and brought him in. Now he was ruddy, with
bright eyes, and good-looking. And
the Lord said, "Arise, anoint him; for
this is the one!" ¹³ Then Samuel took the
horn of oil and anointed him in the midst of
his brothers; and the Spirit of the Lord came
upon David from that day forward. So
Samuel arose and went to Ramah.

1 Samuel 16:11-13

Not only was David passionate about caring
for the sheep; he loved God with a passion,
too. He worshiped God so freely that his
wife Michal was upset with him (2 Samuel
6:15-23).

David was a lover of God. What takes
priority in your life? Is it God or something
else? Is your job more important than God?
Your career cannot be more important than
God. David loved God so much that he was
not comfortable living in a house while the
Ark was kept in a tent. David wanted to
build God a house. This showed how much
he loved God and had Him as his priority.

Now it came to pass, when David was dwelling in his house, that David said to Nathan the prophet, "See now, I dwell in a house of cedar, but the ark of the covenant of the Lord is under tent curtains."

1 Chronicles 17:1

In the book of Haggai, the case was reversed: The people were more interested in building their houses instead of restoring the temple. The exiles were now returning from Babylon, and the foundation of the temple was laid, but, because of opposition from enemies, it was never completed. Sixteen years later it was still in ruin, and God was not happy.

Today some of us are building our kingdom instead of the Kingdom of God. We are focused on creating our own empires instead of focusing on winning souls and growing people in the things of God.

David wanted to build a temple for the Lord. David's heart was right in what he wanted to do, but the Lord had not called him to do that. Nathan the prophet saw it as a good thing and did not inquire of the Lord. He told David to go ahead and do it.

The Lord sent a message back that it was not David but Solomon that would build the temple.

There is a lesson here for us: We must not get so familiar with God that we feel we know His heart in an issue without checking with him. Praise God for people that know how to retract what they have said or done when they realize it is the wrong thing. Nathan went back to David to make amends based on what the Lord said to him.

God does not need a house today built with the hand of man; He lives in us as His temple (church). Do you as His church run around the whole day only to say a quick prayer at night before you go to bed? Do you give time daily to worship, study of the Word, and prayer?

We understand David did. You have to cultivate a life style of worship, prayer, study, and meditation of the Word. I believe in having a set time to commune with the Lord on a daily basis. I know how cranky I get if I miss my time with God.

It takes being intentional sometimes to stay in His presence because many distractions come to take our focus away. "In His presence is fullness of joy." You cannot be part of His church and have no time for Him. We are His bride. How can I not have time for my husband?

We hear of relationship breakdowns with ministers because the husband or wife is too busy with the ministry affairs that they have little or no time for each other. If we do not have time for Him, there will eventually be a breakdown that may bring about permanent damage to us and to the Body.

The pastor comes on Sunday to motivate the congregation. He is able to arouse the soul while the heart remains unchanged.

At a Spirit-led church, the people in the congregation come on Sunday without prayer, and, when the word of the Lord searches their hearts, they become offended and leave the church, instead of asking the Spirit of God to reveal areas that need change in their lives.

Some ministers no longer preach on holiness because it offends the people. Holiness is still applicable today, and the Lord is Holy. It is because we could not live up to God's standard that Jesus came to redeem us. We are under grace today, but grace does not mean we continue a lifestyle of sin.

The Church cannot lower God's standard just because we want to fit in and be accepted. He did not tell us to fit in; He calls us to stand out. We are a peculiar people.

It was evident that the presence of the Lord was with David because whenever Saul was tormented by an evil spirit, David played the harp for him and he was relieved.

We as His Church are called to bring deliverance to the captive. People in the world should come to the Church to seek help, and, when they come, we are to manifest the power of God. When they find the solution for their issue in the church, it gives us an opportunity to introduce that person to Jesus, who is the burden bearer and our peace.

David was bold. Goliath had been terrorizing the children of Israel, and no one could fight him. David fought Goliath and defeated him with a sling and with a stone (1 Samuel 17:31-58). David did not go after the giant in his own strength; he went against him in the name of the Lord.

The Church with this kind of mindset will do exploits for God. She knows that in her own strength she cannot achieve anything. Attention is never drawn to her but to the Lord. They are true worshippers of God.

Saul wanted David to wear his armor, but David knew the armor would not help him. The Lord would.

16 No king is saved by the multitude of an army; A mighty man is not delivered by great strength.

Psalm 33:16

*6 For I will not trust in my bow,
Nor shall my sword save me.*

Psalm 44:6

David had a rough journey before getting to the throne. He was anointed at a very young age and then reigned over Judah for seven years and six months. The fulfillment of the prophecy that he would be King over Israel came to pass when he was thirty years old **(2 Samuel 5:4-5)**.

The Church should wait on the fulfillment of the promise of God over the Church. There is a mandate for each person as His Church as well as the Body of Believers. If we wait on His timing, we gain all the experience we need to gain and we are strengthened.

David could have acceded to the throne more quickly by killing Saul when he had the opportunity. But he did not do that because David believed that, if God anointed him to be king, God would raise him to the throne.

The Lord called my husband and I to start a church by the name of Harvestland International Christian Center. I must say it has been very challenging, but we have seen God's miraculous hand in this ministry. There are times, though, that we have felt that certain people might be able to help get the ministry off the ground, especially in those moments that we seem not to know what else to do. Every fleshly effort we made proved futile. We end up going back to waiting for Him. May you never get too desperate that you leave Him out of the picture?

He sometimes will ask me, "Are you the one building the church or me?"   I am learning to rest in the assurance of His Word. He gave the vision for the church and the name. If He does not want to accomplish something with the church, He would not have set it in place.

He expects us as His church to enter into His rest. David was able to do that, and God showed Himself faithful to David.

He is asking us as His church to let Him do the building. We need to consult with Him in those times when we are unsure. Some things may look good to do to help move us forward as the body, but it may not be the God thing.

After the death of Saul and Jonathan, David did not run off to get into the palace. David inquired of the Lord. Even after the Lord told him to go up, David went further to ask the Lord for the specific place.

David had seen so many things unfold during his waiting period that he needed to make sure he was walking in full obedience as far as the next step. My prayer is that as the church of Jesus Christ we would learn not to lean on our own understanding but acknowledge God in all of our ways

David walked in humility. He saw Saul as God's anointed and therefore said nothing bad about him nor ever tried to hurt him,

even when he had the opportunity, as we
said earlier.

David could have justified his killing of Saul
as self-defense, because Saul was after his
life. There are three lessons to learn here.

- David knew what God spoke
  concerning his life, and God, who
  chose him when he was not looking
  for the position, promised to sustain
  him and accomplish His purpose
  through him.

- At the same time, David did not put
  himself in harms' way. He ran away
  from danger.

- Some of you may have been hurt by
  people in leadership position. It is
  not your job to avenge, and it is not
  healthy to allow the root of bitterness
  to develop. Let God work things out
  for you. To read more on this and
  how to see the good in the bad, read
  my book on The Road to Destiny,
  Updated Version.

Some of our churches are struggling
spiritually, but they're still going on as if
nothing is wrong. We need to seek God to
find out what we need to do differently.

Samson took for granted the anointing on his life. Through Delilah, the woman he was going about with, the enemy finally found out that the secret of his power was his hair. His hair was shaved and he no longer had any power. They cut his hair while he was drunk and asleep.

Samson woke up thinking he still had the power; he was going to shake himself like before, but then he noticed the power of God had left him. Like Samson, some of the churches are still shaking themselves trying to live on past glory. It is time to retrace our steps and seek God again.

14 If My people who are called by My name will humble themselves, and pray and seek My face, and turn from their wicked ways, then I will hear from heaven, and will forgive their sin and heal their land. 15 Now My eyes will be open and My ears attentive to prayer made in this place.
2 Chronicles 7:14-15

I was in a church service once when the pastor said, "I know for sure I hear God once a year or maybe two or three times to be precise." Who leads the church the rest of the year?

Chapter 6

The Saul-Mindset Church: People Pleaser

It is about pleasing the people. Saul stepped into a priesthood role because Samuel delayed in coming. He did not want them to be angry with him (1 Samuel 15). He feared man more than he feared God.

Saul, because he heard nothing from God, consulted with a witch to bring up the spirit of Samuel for him to ask questions. This is what happens when we walk in rebellion due to disobedience.

It was an abomination to consult with a witch. The scripture in the Old Testament says, "Suffer not a witch to live." Saul was the one that sent the witches out of town (1 Samuel 28:9). He now went to consult with one of the people that he banished. One act of disobedience will lead to another if we do not repent. Second, Saul disobeyed God by not killing King Agag. He also took some animals, even though he was instructed to kill them. He took them instead as spoils of war. Third, he went to consult with a medium because God was no longer answering him.

Obedience is better than sacrifice. Scripture promises that, if we are obedient, we will eat the good of the land.

Moses understood the importance of God's presence; he refused to go anywhere without God's presence with them. We will enjoy His presence more if we choose to walk in obedience.

God has made a home in you. We are His temple now. He is constructing the building. The Head directs the body. Imagine it being possible to survive with a missing head. How would one see, smell, eat, hear, and talk? The rest of the body would eventually die due to lack of nourishment and the ability to use the five senses.

The people are not the head of the church; Jesus is. And He is the one that supplies all we need.

"Christ is also the head of the church, which is his body. He is the beginning, supreme over all who rise from the dead. So he is

first in everything. [19] For God in all his fullness was pleased to live in Christ"

NLT **Colossians 1:18-19**

Jesus said, "I am the Light of the world." If Jesus is light, why do we dim the natural light? The World needs to see His light radiating through us. This is what came to my spirit: the dimming of the natural light is a manifestation of what is happening to part of the Body. The light is getting dim.

Jesus is the answer for the world today. There are not many ways to God. Jesus is the **ONLY** Way. There are not many Gods. There is only one God, and He is Jehovah. He is the Creator of the universe. He is the only one that remains eternally the same.

We need to stop trying to please people. We are to please God. We are building The Kingdom of God, not the kingdom of man. Therefore focus on doing what He tells you to do. God told Jeremiah not to look at the faces of the people but focus on the assignment. If you focus on people and their reaction, you will miss God. I pray it will not be your portion in Jesus name.

Jesus said we cannot have two masters; we will love one and hate the other. If we choose to please the people, we cannot please the Master. Usually the demands of the Master will be contrary to what most people want.

If we have cultivated an environment that is less threatening, how effective has that been in terms of changed lives? And how has that manifested the power of God to heal and deliver?

We have beautiful buildings: People come every Sunday and leave unchanged. We gather a crowd, but how many of these people are ready for Heaven?

The people Saul tried to please cost him the kingdom. As we said earlier, this is the same thing that happened to Moses. He was so frustrated by the attitude and complaint of the people that he disobeyed the Lord's instruction, and, because of this, he did not enter the promise land. God allowed him to see it, but he could not enter. This shows how important obedience is to the Lord.

There are some things we can glean from others that may help the Kingdom of God to expand. But if we want expansion so we can boast of having a big church, our priorities are misplaced.

Another aspect of Saul was his jealousy of David. David came and killed Goliath. David had relationship with the Lord even though he was just a shepherd boy on the field. He knew God to be the God of Power and Might. Because of this, he was not afraid to face a seemingly impossible situation. The people were so proud of what he accomplished.

They came up with a song: "David had killed his ten thousands and Saul his thousands." Saul became jealous of David. When Saul was being tormented by an evil spirit, he called on David. Every time David played the instrument, the evil spirit left Saul. Saul wanted to use David for his own agenda without wanting David to grow and enlarge.

This also is another area of the church where a person with the Saul type of mindset will use the people under him as a leader to expand his kingdom instead of the Kingdom of God. The kingdom of God is bigger than any one man, and there is enough room for each person to express their God-given gift.

If you are not a member of the worship team, it does not mean you cannot sing and worship God. Some people are more anointed based on the gifting on their lives. As a Child of God, there is something in you, and do not allow man to belittle what God has given you.

David killed Goliath and played the harp, which brought relief to Saul from the evil spirit tormenting him, but Saul was still out to kill David because of Jealousy. Keep God in the center of all you do, and your gift will eventually make room for you. With all Saul did to try to kill David, and so kill the destiny of David, God was still with David all the way.

The day I got saved, I made up my mind that my allegiance is to God first, not to man. I respect authority and will never undermine anyone, but at the same time I do not allow man to undermine what God has on my life.

I strive daily for a closer walk with God. If it were not for that, the persecutions I have faced would have driven me away from following God. Sometimes it was very challenging, but, like Peter said, "Where can we go?" Jesus has the Word of eternal life.

I have been asked to prophesy to support the message of the pastor because the people listen to what I have to say. I could not do that and I paid dearly for not going along.

If I did what I was told, I would be sinning against God, speaking out of my soul and saying something He did not ask me to say. I would also be betraying the trust and the respect of the people that believe in the Word of the Lord which He puts in my mouth to speak.

"Make the Lord of Heaven's Armies holy in your life. He is the one you should fear. He is the one who should make you tremble."

Isaiah 8:13 (NLT)

Abraham, Daniel, The Hebrew Boys, Joseph, the Disciples and many others feared God. It cost them something to stand for God and what they believed rather than compromise by lowering their standards to please man. They were all honored for doing that.

Some were martyred for standing for God, but they have their reward in Heaven. Stephen, while being stoned to death for speaking the word of truth and for being full of the Spirit and faith, saw Jesus standing to welcome Him into Heaven. It was worth the persecution he suffered.

As you continue to keep God's standard, you will be honored, He will continue to grace you for great things in Jesus name.

Chapter 7

The Ascension Gifts

¹¹ Now these are the gifts Christ gave to the church: the apostles, the prophets, the evangelists, and the pastors and teachers. ¹² Their responsibility is to equip God's people to do his work and build up the church, the body of Christ. ¹³ This will continue until we all come to such unity in our faith and knowledge of God's Son that we will be mature in the Lord, measuring up to the full and complete standard of Christ. ¹⁴ Then we will no longer be immature like children. We won't be tossed and blown about by every wind of new teaching. We will not be influenced when people try to trick us with lies so clever they sound like the truth.¹⁵ Instead, we will speak the truth in love, growing in every way more and more like Christ, who is the head of his body, the church. ¹⁶ He makes the whole body fit together perfectly. As each part does its own special work, it helps the other parts grow, so that the whole body is healthy and growing and full of love."

Ephesians 4:11-19 (NLT)

The five-fold Ministries are Christ's Gift to His Church. They are builders of the Kingdom of God. They achieve this by building others up. They do not try to build a kingdom for themselves. They train and equip the saints to reach their full potential and maturity in Christ.

If you function in one of the offices and have no desire to train the people to mature in their gift and grow more in love with Jesus, something is wrong. There are many good books out there dealing with the Ascension Gifts; if you want an in depth study, you can purchase one of them.

For this book, I am only scratching the surface. The book would not be complete without alluding to them. These gifts cannot function outside of the grace of God upon the lives of those who have them. No man can ordain you into this office. Christ Himself calls the people.

If you were asked to share your experience of how the Lord called you, will you have something to share? Or will all you have to say is, "I was just ordained into the office"?

The Apostle – Builds and governs
The Prophet – Provides hunger for the word of God and guides.
The Teacher – Instructs us in the word of God.
The Pastor – Is called to nurture and love the church. These are the Shepherds.
The Evangelist – Tells us about the good news of the death and resurrection of Christ. They are gatherers of the people..

Each is needed in the Body for us to reach full maturity.

As one that is called, you are to flow with the heart of God in what you do, and you are to love His people. You cannot choose only to go to places where you know they will financially bless you. That temptation may be always present, but we must remember that we are working for Jesus and that He will reward us. The important thing is to know you are going to where He called you to go.

If you live based on what you are able to get, that is a shame. I know of a pastor who will have lunch only with visitors or new members that he knows are rich and will bring in a lot of money. The ones without money cannot get an audience with him.

This is contrary to the heart of God and the call on your life. God is no respecter of persons. None of us qualified for his mercy, but he chose to extend His mercy to us.

"My brethren, do not hold the faith of our Lord Jesus Christ, the Lord of glory, with partiality. ² For if there should come into your assembly a man with gold rings, in fine apparel, and there should also come in a poor man in filthy clothes, ³ and you pay attention to the one wearing the fine clothes and say to him, "You sit here in a good place," and say to the poor man, "You stand there," or, "Sit here at my footstool," ⁴ have you not shown partiality among yourselves, and become judges with evil thoughts?

James 2:1-4 (NKJV)

This is not just peculiar to the pastor; any of the ascension gifts could be over a church. Some ministers will only go to places where they know the honorarium will be substantial. A church may not be able to afford a big honorarium, but you may have what they need to break through into their next season. Let the Spirit of God guide you in your decision making.

It is possible that the meeting we choose not to go to, because it does not fit the class of meetings we want, may have a future world evangelist at the meeting. A nation shaker, history maker may be there, but you can only get to such if you allow yourself to be led by the spirit.

I also would say the church should also not take guest ministers for granted by exploiting them. They incurred expenses coming to your church, and, if this is what they do full time, they deserve to be blessed, too. Always know what you want to give before the minister gets there. You are not to wait on what the offering will be to determine what you will give.

I ministered at a church some time ago, and this was from the testimony of the pastor later. After the meeting, the Spirit of the Lord told him to write the check for a certain amount. He said what they had in the account was not enough but "he recognized it was the voice of His Father." In obedience he did, trusting that when I pay in the check the money will be there somehow. They counted the offering that Sunday, and it was five times the check he wrote. He said they had never received such a large offering before.

It did not stop there. The pastor's car was so old that he felt it was better to just take public transportation than continue to use the car. It was costing too much to keep it running. Tuesday of that same week, one of the members turned forty. For her gift the husband bought her a brand new car. She believed she heard the Lord tell her to give it to her pastor. She gave the brand new car to her pastor. Obedience to the voice of the Lord has its reward. Imagine if the pastor had disobeyed the voice; who knows if God would still have blessed him the way he did.

This is why it is important to listen to His voice. We always tell people who give in the service outside of the tithe. Do not do more or less than what He tells you to do. Sometimes logically it makes no sense.

Mary said to the servants at the wedding in Cana of Galilee when they ran out of wine to do whatever Jesus told them to do. Jesus told them to fill the jugs with water and to draw out of it and give to the guests. The people did not see the water turn to wine before drawing it; they obeyed Him and the miracle occurred.

My prayer for you and for me is that the Lord will give us the grace not to lose focus of who our provider is in Jesus name.

Everything we do, we do as unto the Lord. He put the gifts in the church and we have to learn to honor the gifts so we can enjoy the grace on their lives.

When a guest is invited to our meeting, we already have in mind what the Lord would have us bless the person with regardless of what the offering is. We do not give less than what we know we are to give. That is honoring the vessel. If you sow from what you have with sincerity of heart, you will reap the same.

We should not make unreasonable demands from the people.

The brother of our pastor some years ago shared with us how their church invited a minister to come and minister there. The minister faxed a list of what he would need before he can come. I cannot fully remember everything but I do remember him saying the minister demanded a five star hotel and a limousine. The brother of our pastor said he faxed back saying, 'I think we have the wrong man.''

We are losing focus with all these demands. We are forgetting that we are Christ's bond servant. We are called to serve. Jesus washed the feet of His disciples to show us that we must have a servant's heart.

Why must it be a limousine? We need to ask the question, would Jesus request a limousine if He were here today? He blended so well with his disciples that Judas had to point him out. We cannot be greater or bigger than Jesus. He humbled himself to the death on the cross and was crucified naked for you and for me. He said we should store up our treasures in heaven where moths cannot touch it.

Why are we becoming too earth-focused? Ministers are competing against ministers. Why? Are we not working for the same Kingdom? If Christ as the Head of the Church is the one we take our orders from, there can be no conflict of interest because He will not contradict Himself.

The church must retrace her path, to do what we are called to do. We are to be salt and light in this dark world. We cannot afford to lose our saltiness if this world is to see the light.

Zechariah was a priest who in his old age was promised a son (Luke 1:5-25). As a priest he ought to understand the ways of God. He was in the temple one day when the angel appeared to him with the announcement that his aged wife would have a son. He could not believe that, and, because of his unbelief, he was made mute by the angel until the baby was born.

He knew what God had done in the past, but, with age, he did not see how they both could be parents to a child. He must have forgotten the story of Abraham and Sarah.

Some Churches are set in the way things are now, while God is trying to let them know there is a better way.

The Word of the Lord is the only thing that can bring revival to His Church. The Word of the Lord is what changed the situation of Zechariah and Elizabeth.

The education we acquire, the strategies we learn from seminars, summits, etc., are not enough to bring lasting change. The people may gain more knowledge, but it will not revive the Spirit. Read the word of Jesus in John 6.

"The Spirit alone gives eternal life. Human effort accomplishes nothing. And the very words I have spoken to you are spirit and life."

John 6:63 (NLT)

Lord, help us to look beyond what we see to what you say concerning your church.

Chapter 8

Going Forward

• Unity Brings Power and Manifestation

At the Tower of Babel, the people were trying to build a tower that would reach up to heaven, and the Lord said there is nothing this people cannot achieve if they continue to go the way they are going because they are of one language **(Genesis 11:1-8)**.

When Jesus truly becomes the ruling Head of His church, there will be unity in the Body. When there is unity, we become one voice for Him. We may have different denominations, but it will be one Body striving for the same goal, to see Jesus glorified.

We lift Him up at every opportunity so He can draw men unto Himself. If we let Him reign in our own lives, we are drawn closer to him.

When a member of His Body falls, it should grieve your heart, just as it grieves the heart of the Father. We cannot rejoice in the stumbling of a brother or sister but instead, should pray for his or her restoration.

"Brethren, if a man is overtaken in any trespass, you who are spiritual restore such a one in a spirit of gentleness, considering yourself lest you also be tempted."

Galatians 6:1

Jesus is a restorer of dignity and hope. We have His heart. We are to make decisions based on what He will do.

He wants His Church to be united. That was His prayer in John 17:

"I do not pray for these alone, but also for those who will believe in Me through their word; [21] that they all may be one, as You, Father, are in Me, and I in You; that they also may be one in Us, that the world may believe that You sent Me. [22] And the glory which You gave Me I have given them, that they may be one just as We are one."

John 17:20-22

The Body of Christ must look away from our differences and focus on what is the common bond. Our focus should be on Jesus. If we all believe John 14:6, we are moving in the right direction.

⁶Jesus said to him, "I am the way, the truth, and the life. No one comes to the Father except through Me."

John 14:6

You may be part of a different denomination, but you are still part of the Body of Christ Universal as long as we believe in Him. Our gifts and callings may be different, but it is in us all working together that we can reach full maturity.

⁴ For as we have many members in one body, but all the members do not have the same function, ⁵ so we, being many, are one body in Christ, and individually members of one another.⁶ Having then gifts differing according to the grace that is given to us, let us use them: if prophecy, let us prophesy in proportion to our faith; ⁷ or ministry, let us use it in our ministering; he who teaches, in teaching; ⁸ he who exhorts, in exhortation; he who gives, with liberality; he who leads, with diligence; he who shows mercy, with cheerfulness.

Romans 12:4-8

• The Shepherd

"I am the good shepherd. The good shepherd gives His life for the sheep. [12] But a hireling, he who is not the shepherd, one who does not own the sheep, sees the wolf coming and leaves the sheep and flees; and the wolf catches the sheep and scatters them. [13] The hireling flees because he is a hireling and does not care about the sheep. [14] I am the good shepherd; and I know My sheep, and am known by My own. [15] As the Father knows Me, even so I know the Father; and I lay down My life for the sheep.

John 10:11-15

The Pastor or the set man of the house must take care of the sheep. As one with the ascension gift, you are called to train the members of the Body you oversee to reach their full potential in Christ. Your children should do better than you, because they are combining the grace from you with the one God puts on their lives.

When you see people that are matured and ready to go, you are to release them and not be upset that they have to go. Remember that they belong to Christ.

Jesus taught the disciples and released them into ministry. When you release people under you to walk in their purpose, you are actually enlarging your territory, not diminishing it. Those people leave as sons and daughters from your house. You will remain their spiritual parent.

Do not become a king who castrates his spiritual children by wanting to keep them with you permanently. You must be able to release those who are called to do other things with a Fathers blessing.

Our three children are gifted differently and each one has helped me at different times when I get stuck in different areas.

The last one is very good with technology; I do not bother trying to figure out things that are complicated; I just call him to work on it for me.

One is artistic. When I need to be creative, I ask for his input. Our daughter is more the detailed one and enjoys reading, analyzing, pushing you beyond your limit. When we need to make a purchase, we ask her to research it for us. When I need a different view, I talk with her.

I have seen my husband struggle with things sometimes and it almost gets to a point of frustration, I usually just say to him, "Why don't you call Josh [our son] to fix it for you?" He eventually does and the problem is solved.

I have the opportunity to mentor people in the prophetic all the time. Some were unsure of their gift at the beginning. However, with months of mentoring, I am amazed to see how God has brought out the gift in them. I am now blessed by them speaking words of encouragement to me.

I was at a meeting and one of them ministered. She acknowledged me as her teacher. I watched her minister and I was so blessed. I said "the teacher has become the student."

I am jealous *for* the sons and daughters I have been able to mentor, but never jealous *of* them. There are times that I am discouraged and I call one of them to pray for me. That person ends up encouraging me.

You cannot become an oppressor of your people like Saul was. You are called to love and serve the people of God. God so loved

the world that He gave His only son as a
sacrificial lamb for our redemption.
When love becomes your motivating factor
as His church, you will see people
differently. You will see them as having
been accepted in the beloved. He says
anyone that touches us touches the apple of
His eyes. I do not know if you have ever
stopped to think about that every time a
child of God is oppressed or abused by a
leader. The person is messing with the apple
of God's eye.

• The Sheep

Sheep who are disgruntled sit in their own
counsel and crucify the shepherd. David is a
perfect example of how to deal with a Saul.

David knew he was anointed and nothing
could take that away from. He would one
day become king. He suffered many things
at the hand of Saul, but he never cursed
Saul. When he had the opportunity to kill
Saul, he did not do it.

There is an appointed time, called the
fullness of time, for you. God will bring you
out.

16 A man's gift makes room for him, And brings him before great men.

Proverbs 18:16

You should focus on pleasing Jesus as your Head. One of the ways you please Him is to submit to authority as unto the Lord.

When you become part of a body of believers, you must submit to the authority there. You cannot have your own group of people doing things contrary to the vision of the church. If you feel it is not the place for you, you should leave rather than rebel. Rebellion is as the sin of witchcraft.

Jesus Christ, the Head of the Church, humbled Himself to the death on the cross and God raised him to the place of highest honor.

God will raise you up as you humble yourself.

10 Humble yourselves in the sight of the Lord, and He will lift you up.

James 4:10

When we moved from the Church where we started, we decided to go to a bigger church where we could just sit towards the back and go home after service without anyone noticing us.

After two visits, someone came to where we sat to tell us we were not brought to that church to hide. Oh, my! I was really disappointed.

I find myself in places I could not have been on my own. The doors would never have opened, but the gift of God in me makes room for me. You are the building; He is building. And, if you will let Him continue with it, you will become the best you can be in Him. You will become a vessel of honor in the hand of the Master.

I am learning daily to rely on Him through the leading of His Spirit. Sometimes it has not been easy, especially when things are very challenging. I just want to jump ahead and do something. The times I have done that, it failed, and this feeling of shame came over me. It was not because He said something to me, but because I know I should not have taken the step I took to work things out by myself. I am thankful that when I repent He forgives.

When the Body steps out of line, we remember:

14 if My people who are called by My name will humble themselves, and pray and seek My face, and turn from their wicked ways, then I will hear from heaven, and will forgive their sin and heal their land. 15 Now My eyes will be open and My ears attentive to prayer made in this place.

2 Chronicles 7:14-15

When we go before God in repentance, we do not say the people have sinned. Lord, we have sinned. Daniel and Nehemiah did not separate themselves from the people when they prayed the prayer of repentance.

There is this song that usually blesses me, sung by Robert Gray:

"There is one Body, we have one Lord, United in the spirit, we are going forth. With His praises on our lips and a sword in our hands, We are marching on with power as we possess the land. We are the people of the Lord We are a holy nation, a chosen generation Called to show forth His praise

We are the people of the Lord, we're a holy nation, Believers in Jesus, lifting up our voices to the Lord."

Unity in the Body, as previously discussed, will make this song a reality in our lives. Let us submit our agenda to the Master and take up His. When we submit, we make our agenda of less importance. When we focus on seeking His Kingdom and Righteousness in the Body, He will add all other things to us.

Joshua closed out his ministry in the Book of Joshua with these words:

*[15] And if it seems evil to you to serve the Lord, choose for yourselves this day whom you will serve, whether the gods which your fathers served that were on the other side of the River, or the gods of the Amorites, in whose land you dwell. **But as for me and my house, we will serve the Lord."***

Joshua 24:15

You have a choice to make for the next season you are going into: If you are just doing your own thing; it is time to choose whom you will serve. We can ask him for what we need if we abide in him.

7 If you abide in Me, and My words abide in you, you will ask what you desire, and it shall be done for you.

John 15:7

Chapter 9

Conclusion

We can see things are rounding up and we have to do what we can while it is still day because the night is coming when none of us can work.

God needs the harvest now, and the field is ripe ready for harvesting. We can do much more gathering if we follow God's strategy, and this is the Heart of Jesus. He wants to build for us, not us build for Him, because anything the flesh builds will eventually die.

Church services have become so regimented in some of our meetings that the Spirit of God has no freedom of expression anymore. We sing three songs and go to the next thing on the agenda. We come from Sunday to Sunday and just do the same thing all over again.

What do we do if we come into service and the Lord says no sermon today, just worship? We will be confused because God just messed up our agenda.

As we yield going forward, we will see more of His movement and manifestation. We cannot time a timeless God. Sometimes, God is just about to start when we are about to leave.

I do understand that, in the name of the Holy Spirit, He is moving, just going on and on. We have to learn to quit when He stops.

There are times I am giving a message and the Spirit of God will tell me it is enough, go into time of ministry. I just stop and go into ministry time. What is the essence of continuing to talk, when the anointing has been lifted on the message and moved on to the next thing on God's heart?

Let us read the words of Jesus, The Head of the Church:

"For I have come down from heaven, not to do My own will, but the will of Him who sent Me. 40And this is the will of Him who sent Me, that everyone who sees the Son and believes in Him may have everlasting life; and I will raise him up at the last day."

John 6:38, 40

If anyone wills to do His will, he shall know concerning the doctrine, whether it is from God or whether I speak on My own authority. 18He

who speaks from himself seeks his own glory;
but He who seeks the glory of the One who sent
Him is true, and no unrighteousness is in Him.

John 7:17-18

Then Jesus said to those Jews who believed
Him, "If you abide in My word, you are My
disciples indeed. 32And you shall know the
truth, and the truth shall make you free."

John 8:31, 32

"For I have not spoken on My own
authority; but the Father who sent Me gave
Me a command, what I should say and what
I should speak."

John 12:49

35 By this all will know that you are My
disciples, if you have love for one another."

John 13:35

John 13:35 reminds me of an experience I
had a few years ago. I went on a personal
retreat for three days at a retreat ground in
another state. The place has been running for
over three decades. It is free; you just give a
love offering.

We were to be five in my room. One came from France, one from Canada; another was an Ethiopian, and I. The last lady came in close to midnight. She drove over nine hours to get there. It rained all through her drive. She was soaked when she got to the room.

We had turned the lights off. The lady kept fidgeting to find her stuff; you could see her frustration, because she could not find her torch light. I got up and turned the light on for her. The other two ladies got up to help her, too, but the older lady was furious. She told us how she had worked with the original owners of the camp. She said she had traveled the world and had been in ministry for thirty years. She said we had no right to turn the lights on because it was past midnight and lights out was midnight.

The lady who just came in said it was okay; we could turn the lights off, and she would feel her way through her things. That did not sit well with me at all. I asked the lady who had been in ministry for so long, "Do you think Jesus would go to bed while this lady tries to feel her way through in the dark and all wet?" She said nothing else but instead turned her face to the wall.

I actually thought it was over, but the next morning she met me in the kitchen and said it is a privilege for anyone to come here and, if they cannot obey the rules, they need not come, so we had no right turning the light on. Wow, holy anger rose inside me! I told her this lady drove nine hours in the rain; that must be her reason for coming so late. I said, "Jesus was accused of healing on the Sabbath, too, and He said Sabbath was made for man and not man for the Sabbath."

I went further to tell her, "I am sure we did what Jesus would have done."

She later came into the room to apologize. If this is what ministry turns one into, it is best not to go into ministry at all. Character is what will matter at the end of the day. The fruit of the spirit is love. Prophecy and the gifts will cease; only love will endure

Abraham, the Father of the Jews, was an Assyrian before he was chosen and called out by God.

Even though God called him, life was not easy for him. It seemed like things became more challenging for him. When you choose to go all the way in obedience to God's instruction, some will think you have lost it.

But, if you stay faithful, it will pay off in the end. It did for Abraham. Our God is called the God of Abraham, and scripture says he was a friend of God.

Saul, on the other hand, could not walk in full obedience, and it cost him the throne. Half obedience is no obedience at all.

When we came to the Lord, too, we made some enemies, because what was once good was no longer good. Some of the things we did with our friends and the places we went we can no longer go.

It is a privilege to be singled out by God for His purpose. It is not enough to be called; we must follow God with our whole heart.

Nineveh found special favor in the eyes of God. He sent Jonah to warn the people of Nineveh to turn from their wicked ways. They did, and He extended mercy. They turned around and went back into their wickedness and God judged them. God tempers justice with mercy if we repent.

We grope in the dark if we become headless. We become like sheep doing our own thing because we no longer let the Chief Shepherd lead.

If you are facing challenges because of the call of God on your life, it is expected. Do not become faint hearted; be encouraged, knowing He will never leave you nor forsake you.

The Church is coming under greater persecution, but we can stand in the midst of all the trials without compromising if we cultivate intimacy with our Lord. It is in His presence we find fullness of joy, and His joy becomes our strength.

Is your light shining as it should to illuminate the darkness, or, when you get into a dark environment, do you blend in?

The most important thing to know is this, Christ is our Redeemer. No matter how far gone you are, He will forgive if you come back in repentance. God can redeem from homosexual and Lesbian tendencies. He can deliver from adultery, fornication, cheating, lying, etc. If you cry out to the Lord, He will answer you and deliver you.

[15] Call upon Me in the day of trouble; I will deliver you, and you shall glorify Me."

Psalm 50:15

I have observed that, once the focus is shifted from praying in the church, decline starts. We replace prayer with good activities that do nothing for the spirit man. If Jesus rose up early in the morning to pray, how then do we think we can make a success of what He has called us to without prayer?

Some Churches are still very much into prayer and I thank God for them. I am sure we can see the difference in the move of God in these ministries. I am talking about prayer that is geared more towards seeing the will of God accomplished on earth as it is in heaven. It is not just a "give me," "give me," kind of prayer.

We can have the best activities that draw people to the church, but without prayer the Church cannot be powerful. Prayer sets the tone for what happens in the service.

Some go to a church gathering to pacify their conscience, but have not seen or experience the move of God in a long time. We have settled for service with no power. Going to church on the day of worship should be exciting because we are oblivious to how God will move. However, one thing we can be sure of is that it will wonderful and life changing!

In the book of Amos, the Lord said He will do nothing unless He first reveals it to His servants, the prophets. This means there is nothing God is doing upon the earth that is not revealed to one of His vessels somewhere.

God does this so we are not ignorant of what He is doing in the earth. If you avail yourself to Him, there is so much He can share and do with you. Jesus is the answer for the world today. Let us become the vessels that would help in solving the problems faced by people in the world.

They want something that the world cannot give to them. There is a void, an emptiness that only a relationship with Jesus can fill. Some of them may not know why they go to a church. The desire for something more is what leads them to the building, though they may not realize it.

The yearning and the seeking will continue because man-made program cannot achieve God-ordained result. It is God's goodness (kindness) that leads a man to repentance.

This is why it is imperative that we make Jesus known to them

"Or do you despise the riches of His goodness, forbearance, and longsuffering, not knowing that the goodness of God leads you to repentance?"

Romans 2:4

• **Accountability**

David had a repentant heart; he was able to admit his sin of adultery with Bathsheba. He sought forgiveness from the Lord. We must have people in our lives that we can talk to and be transparent with when we find things are wrong. We seek the Lord's forgiveness first.

David tried at first to cover up his deed, but the Lord uncovered it because of His love for him. Those He loves, He corrects.

I believe the Lord does not just expose things. He gives the person room to repent by sending many warnings, but, if not heeded, it becomes an open shame.

Sometimes it may be a marital struggle that may require you to talk with someone who can counsel and pray with you. It may be frustration in ministry. You need to talk with someone before the enemy takes advantage.

It is so painful when I hear of ministers of the gospel committing suicide. The Lord did not create you an island. Please, whenever you feel you are unable to bear it any longer, find someone you trust that you can talk with after praying. Encouragement from another person will do you good.

I was talking with a lady once and she said in our church we cannot afford to speak or make open our challenges. We have been taught to always put up a front that things are okay. This is not acceptable, because it is the quickest way to fall into depression.

Be encouraged knowing the best is yet to come. You are part of the army. Remain vigilant and sensitive to His Voice. I pray that your destiny will not be cut short. Your days you will fulfill in Jesus name.

I hope you have been blessed by this. The church is getting into exiting times. Jesus wins in the end. I would love to hear from you on what God is doing differently in your life if you have decided to champion His cause.

*Jesus, remain the head of Your Church.
We repent of our "do-it-yourself" spirit. We
surrender our all to you!*

Chosen Remnant Christian Ministries
P. O. Box 800,
Powder Springs, GA 30127
chosenremnant@gmail.com
margaretsowemimo@gmail.com

www.chosenremnant.org
www.harvestlandicc.org

www.ingramcontent.com/pod-product-compliance
Lightning Source LLC
Chambersburg PA
CBHW031558040426
42452CB00006B/347